# WHERE HAVE WE COME FROM, WHERE ARE WE GOING?

By Mary K Gowdy

*For information contact; address www.marykgowdy.com*

*Book and Cover Design by Alejandrob*

*ISBN-13: 9781734950526*

*First Edition: June 2022*

*10 9 8 7 6 5 4 3 2 1*

# Table of Contents

*To my parents,*
*I know some of this might be hard to read,*
*but I wouldn't be who I am without you two.*

I picked up a pencil and held it over a sheet of white paper, but my feelings stood in the way of my words. Well, I would wait, day and night, until I knew what to say. Humbly now, with no vaulting dream of achieving a vast unity, I wanted to try to build a bridge of words between me and that world outside, that world which was so distant and elusive that it seemed unreal.

I would hurl words into this darkness and wait for an echo, and if an echo sounded, no matter how faintly, I would send other words to tell, to march, to fight, to create a sense of the hunger for life that gnaws in us all, to keep alive in our hearts a sense of the inexpressibly human.

- Richard Wright, *Black Boy*

## 10,000 Hours

Some would say language is art that bridges ideas
split by invisible chasms. Only the skilled few can
reveal the connections between metaphor's two parts.

Others would say language is manipulation
that misleads the humble tourists
into the caves of the skilled few
who enslave them with their fake news and PC rules.

We fear how language can damage deeper than bones
by beautifying and justifying ideas
that shouldn't be condoned.
We want it raw,
presented without dressing like our friends would,
though we all command with the question:
*Can you pass the salt?*

Before a child is learned in words, they cry
to spill into their parents
the message of their hearts, pure and unrestrained.
I wish I could do the same
—make known all that is within me
beyond what words I can say so no one can claim
I pulled them along with my slanted lines
of poetry. But I pick my words precisely
just like those before me
who used them to heal and hurt.

# Rites of Passage

Sitting under lush oaks, my friends and I debate
as we wait for the train. *Racial inequality*
*is definitely still a thing. Socialism would work.*
*We just need to not have money.* When it comes,
we'll board like the other adults
for the first time in our eighteen years
and become true citizens.
It'll take us to cast our first votes.
We're excited. We're grown up now,
have left the optimism of innocence
and accepted the cynicism caused by corruption.
I've consumed the news with my parents, laughed
at the stupidity shown on Watters' World.
For an eighth grade assignment to encourage
the adults to vote, I'd made a poster that had said,
*It's voting. Just do it,* because it's so simple,
like being kind. I'd colored it in
with red, white, and blue because
patriotism, you know.

The train's blaring horn makes me jump
as it slides into the station, belching
clouds of black smoke. Its yellow eye stares out
from its self-created fog. Once it's skidded to a halt,
everyone hurries to the doors as they hiss open.
As I follow, I notice the people
who remain on the ground
and the others who spit on them
because they are too dumb and lazy
to do what is so simple.
*Get on the train!* the conductor yells.

As I near the doors, the crowd's momentum
carries me through. I've lost my friends,
so I call out but no one responds. There are so many
people it seems unlikely anyone will hear me.

## Build Your House Upon the Rock

After my first breaths, my parents taught me
whom they belonged to. When I wasn't yet old
enough to fear death, they taught me
who had saved me from it.
They pointed to pictures of a lion
lying down with a lamb, a man made out of dirt,
a silhouette on a cross. Lounging on the rock
of their faith,

I dip my fingertips into the ocean around me.
A school of minnows nibble at my dead skin.
Each touch reminds me of an act of grace and love
from my parents—at how they've shared, helped,
and forgiven. When I spin my finger to create
a whirlpool of ripples, the water slips from my control

to churn on its own. Shadows prowl in its zone,
and I hear an angry man's mumbling—staticky
like through a bad TV connection. *They—all idiots—*
*destr—ng—merican god—values.—bringing crime.*
*They're ra—. Who—d vote for—ce?*
My dad explains, *They thought Reagan*
*had been crazy, but he did a lot of good things.*
But when I repeat it to my teacher, he says
he hopes not. Blushing, I crouch on the edge
of the rock to hear better. *They're bringing crime,*
says Trump. *They're rapists. Who would vote for that*
*face?*

A strong gust slaps me over,
and I belly-flop into the water.
My feet can't support me because there are chasms

where I thought the bottom of the ocean would be.
I flail towards a rock, worm my way onto its square
foot of sand, gasp the breath back
into my lungs. When I search for my parents' rock,
there's a jagged ridge on its side
I'd never noticed before.
It obscures the place I used to sit.

There's no way to swim back.

# Facts

My friends tell me
*people are idiots at best,*
*racists at worst for supporting*
*those policies, hear the facts*
—their facts,
the reasons they've picked.
When I hear their takes
on objective events,

~ my trust shrivels
like a plant that's lost its sun ~

when my family counters with
*it's not that bad,*
*the government's done that*
*sort of thing before*
—their reasons,
the facts they've been forced
to accept, flake away
my innocence each time they resign
to accept the atrocities done by leaders
new and old.

# The American Guide On How to Formulate Your Own Opinion: Wheel of Fortune Edition

**Host:** From an AP Gov Classroom, it's America's game! Ladies and Gentlemen, here are the stars of our show!

**Mary Katherine Gowdy:** Hi, I'm a senior at Jamison Prep, and I have no idea what I want to do with my life. And I have no beautiful husband or wonderful children. 'Cause I'm only seventeen.

**Ada Palmer:** I'm also a senior at Jamison Prep, and I'm still trying to figure things out too. But I'm interested in social justice and environmentalism. Bernie does have chance, y'all! Feel the Bern 2016!

**Brock Valder:** Yeah, what they said. I'm goin' to Ole Miss, gonna be an orthopedic surgeon. Go Rebels!

**Host:** Let's do our first toss-up. The clue is Foreign Enemy of the United States.

**Brock:** Japan...They're communists, right?

**Ada:** No, that's China.

**Host:** Correct! 2,000 citizenship points to Ada Palmer. Russia was also an acceptable answer. Though, you had the right idea there, Brock. Ada, go ahead and spin that wheel. The clue is The Perfect Economic System.

**Ada:** *spins wheel, lands on Lose a Turn*

**Host:** Aw, sorry about that, Ada. On to you, Mary Katherine. What's your answer?

**Mary Katherine:** ...Did I mention that I don't understand how economics has any basis in reality?

**Host:** *laughs* Come on, answer.

**Mary Katherine:** Well, there's no such thing as a perfect economy. It's just a theoretical concept that can't exist. So it's a trick question! *looks at host expectantly*

**Host:** There is a correct answer, and that is...not it. Onto you, Brock.

**Brock:** Capitalism, obviously.

**Host:** Correct! The answer was America's economy! You're going to the Bahamas, Brock!

**Voice-over:** Kick back and relax as you delight in sunny beaches and—

**Ada:** Excuse me! America is a mixed economy that includes several qualities of socialism, not just capitalism.

**Brock:** Says the socialist supporter. You want to turn our whole country that way!

**Ada:** Bernie's a democratic socialist. There's a difference.

**Voice-over:** —the possibilities are endless. Valued at 7,000 citizenship points!

**Ada:** Capitalism couldn't be the right answer.

**Host:** Spin the wheel, Brock. The clue is The Solution to America's Race Problems.

**Brock:** *spins wheel, lands on Bankrupt*

**Host:** Man, the wheel is not being friendly tonight. Ada, your turn.

**Ada:** *spins wheel, lands on Express*

**Host:** Ooooo, so the way we're going to do this, you have 30 seconds to guess as many possible answers and you get 1,000 citizenship points for each correct one. Are you ready?

**Ada:** Oh, I've been ready. *cracks knuckles*

**Host:** The timer starts. Now.

**Ada:** Affordable housing, more funding for the school districts of largely minority communities, end gerrymandering, more social programs to raise people out of poverty, end police brutality and the prison industrial complex that mostly imprisons black men and takes away their right to vote, tax the rich, take away white people's privile—.

**Host:** Time's up. *grimaces* None of those answers are correct I'm afraid. Mary Katherine, spin the wheel.

**Ada:** What! This game is rigged!

**Brock:** If this game was rigged, I, as a white male, wouldn't be bankrupted right now.

**Ada:** Shut up! Your dad will bail you out.

**Mary Katherine:** *spins wheel, lands on 1200 citizenship points* Uh, I don't know. It's a pretty complex issue, and I'm white so I don't know a lot about what goes on in the black community. Or how to help them.

**Host:** *chuckles uncomfortably, holds up cards to cover his mouth and whispers to Mary Katherine* We're trying to help you grow into a responsible, mature citizen here. You have to know what you believe about these important issues.

**Mary Katherine:** But I don't want to give my opinion of something I'm ignorant of.

**Host:** Why would that matter? You don't want to look dumb and uneducated, or be a bad citizen. *glances at Mary Katherine's 0 citizenship points*

**Mary Katherine:** But I don't know what to say.

**Host:** Is that your final answer?

**Mary Katherine:** Yeah, whatever.

**Host:** That is incorrect, sorry. Onto you, Brock.
**Brock:** *spins wheel, lands on 1 million citizenship points wedge* We need to put more funding into the police, not less. Most of African Americans' troubles stem from black-on-black crime. There would just be chaos if we didn't support our men in blue who put their lives on the line everyday dealing with these poorer minority communities.

**Host:** Pick up that 1 million citizenship point wedge!

**Brock:** *waves the wedge above his head and yells with a pumped fist*

**Ada:** Bulls@#!

**Host:** Watch your language, young miss. We're in a private school.

**Ada:** I told you it was rigged! You're giving him everything!

*bell rings*

**Host:** Oh, looks like we're running out of time. Let's do our last toss-up. The clue is Who is the Presidential Candidate Who Will Fix Our Nation's Problems? *spins wheel, lands on 4,000*

**Ada:** Bernie!

**Host:** It has to be someone who will actually be in the general election.

**Brock:** Trump!

**Host:** That is correct! You'll be going to our bonus round!

**Mary Katherine:** *rips off her microphone and leaves the stage*

**Host:** What are you doing, Miss Gowdy?

**Mary Katherine:** I'm done with this game. I quit.

**Brock:** Good. You weren't winning anything anyway.

**Host:** But we have the rest of the semester. The rest of your life. You can't...quit? Does that mean you're not going to vote? Not every country gives its citizens the right to elect their officials.

**Mary Katherine:** I don't know. I just...need some time to clear my head. To learn more about the world.

**Brock:** *goes off-stage to celebrate his win with his family*

**Ada:** *jumps on Brock's back to wrestle him to the ground* You cheated! The system was rigged so that you would win!

**Brock:** *throws Ada off his back* What are you talkin' about! I earned this, bitch!

**Mary Katherine:** *leaves, grimacing at the scene*

**Ada:** *pushes over stage lights and microphones so they smack into the crew, goes up to scream into camera* People of America, you must know what's really going on in our educational system today. They won't let us women and minorities win! We have to band toge—.

**Host:** *pushes Ada away to get into the camera frame* Shut it of—.

OFF AIR — PLEASE STAND BY

## America First

Trump's
campaign
promises to keep
America first above
all. Around his pulpit, his supporters
cheer, hoping he will rescue their nation
back to its former glory and
reign under the God who
said that the last
shall be
first.

# Why I Didn't Vote in the Election of 2016

My peers demand action.
Make a stand, take a step       towards their vision.
I fumble along facts, news, truths, values,
not sure what I am following.


Pour yourself into the page, they say.
Cast your vote.       Get it out.
All your anxiety, your faith into this ink stain
so you may wake to catharsis,
sweaty and comforting on your skin.
No guilt for walking past the poor
on the street       till the next ballot.


I cannot sleep
for the weak whispers of the drowned
cry to me, their voices cracked with salt.
They ask how can we rely on pen scratches
on paper to fix these horrors. Their lungs
know no difference
between inept saviors and none.
They wait for my voice,


but the knowledge of my ignorance unravels me
till I can't tie two thoughts together into a belief.
I keep them hidden and don't react
when my peers speak their truth
for it to echo in their abyss.
I close my eyes and ears
to keep the taste of hate off my lips.

## SJWs

Online, the wolf pursues her prey
to strike at any threat—a word,
misstep, or lie. She chokes airways
and rips out guts so that she's heard.
But when she's done, she strips herself
of snout and claws and leaves to dwell
with head on shepherd's lap. He strokes
her fleece and tells her where to go.

## The Metaphors We Live By

You drive me mad as I get lost
in a mirror maze of you in my mind,
and I scream 'cause I fear losing you.

Come dance with me, I don't wanna fight.
Don't marshal your points to defeat me
or shoot down my arguments,
for your blows strike too deep.

I want to hurt you
for not being whom I thought you could be.
I have to choose to stay near, to stay open,
read the stars, steer the rudder,
for I would not reach our shore safely tonight
swept by the waves of pain.

Is love a choice or is it madness?

If it is madness and I am mad, let me fall for and from you,
and if it is a choice and I am the sailor, let my actions love,
for my heart cannot listen, give, or hold you.

Please, come dance with me,
I don't wanna fight.
Don't you see
as long as you're chasing victory
you have to accept the terms of war?

Come dance with me.
Instead of a battle of wits
to overthrow each other's opinions,
where would we be if this debate were a dance

that we share
to lead, follow, fumble, and learn
so we may waltz to a new tune?

# How the Court Jester Became King of the United States

These former debate captains from their fancy
Ivy League schools only learned appeasement,
which made liars of them all.
Money wasted cause money just talks for them
in words bejeweled with alliteration and anaphora
and dressed in the rule of threes.
These pipers' promises turned to dust post-ballot read,
but Trump
barrels through their elite bullshit,
aligns incorrectness with truth.
His wild gestures brand him as the bad boy unrestrained
by society's rules. When the media calls him offensive,
he reminds them that it's bad taste
to critique humor. With a *you're fired*, he promises
swiftness and precision against his opponents. He brings
their visages forth with a slumped, sleepy posture.
*Look at how lazy and slow they are.* He points to himself.
He lassos a rope around the rulers' necks,
drags them through the dirt
till their faces are marred by nicknames
of low energy, little, crooked.
Ascending the steps of bodies
he brought low through debate,
the jester takes the throne.

## November 9, 2016

Donald Trump was elected President of the United States last night. Before I went to bed, he was leading, but I had hoped Hillary would pull through. All day, I had known in my gut that he was going to win somehow. I hadn't wanted to believe it, but I wasn't surprised when I woke up and checked my phone in the middle of the night to see who was the winner.

At dinner on election day, my roommate had told me that everything was going to be the same. We would get up, attend class, and I'd be back in the cafeteria eating rotisserie chicken for dinner like I had since the beginning of the semester. But this morning, I checked my email to make sure we were still having class, that it was safe to attend. Riots and protests in California had already been reported. My classmates expressed their anxiety over the hate crimes they felt were imminent.

When I returned to my dorm, I checked my phone to see that my mom had texted me to check in and remind me that God is in control. I burst into tears on the way to the bathroom. I'd been holding them back all the walk home.

There's no doubt that the votes of Evangelical Christians powered Trump's rise to power. By some miracle, this whole process has made me believe in Christianity more instead of causing me to walk away like my peers. I know the God I was raised to believe in, and he would never support the hateful policies and rhetoric of that man. I know it so deeply like how I knew Trump would win. I have faith in God's sovereignty, but that does not mean some shit isn't about go down. As the Bible says, we are meant to take up our crosses and walk and struggle in this world. By donating money to my church instead of voting, I put my faith in God rather than in man. I keep repeating to myself, "Man cannot save me. God will save me."

In one of my classes, a girl was teary-eyed. She wore all the sorrow that I had had earlier on her face, but with a dose of anger that I don't have. She's terrified. I'm conflicted between thinking rightly so and selfishly wanting someone to tell me that it's going to be okay. I don't think we can be assured of that anymore. The implications of this election cannot be downplayed.

This is the end of the era of Americans deluding themselves into thinking America is greater than it actually is. America portrays itself as a pure nation who always looks out for the oppressed and is the shining light of morality and equality in this world. Yes, we're responsible for "The Shot Heard Around the World," but every step we've taken for equality has also been a step to extricate ourselves from the system built upon slavery, racism, sexism, and xenophobia that we made. We are as responsible for the darkness we have fought against as the light we have produced. We chose to ignore the darkness, seeing the apple as ripening when it is rotten in the core. We can't ignore it anymore. Watergate may have destroyed the previous generation's trust in the government, but the Election of 2016 has destroyed my generation's pride in our nation. We thought we were too progressive of a nation for Trump to even have a chance, and it has devastated us to realize that what we have been taught through propaganda about our nation is a lie. We are confused. Some are angry. And we will never be the same.

I met my roommate for dinner that night and ate rotisserie chicken again. On our way back to our dorm, I gazed up at the stars. The world felt different because the perception of it is created by us and we had become different. But the world does not discontinue being itself. The stars above me have shown down on plantations and lynching trees. It was another day in history. And I returned to my dorm as always to do my homework for the next one.

# Those Who Cannot Remember the Past Are Doomed to Repeat It

When the present events seem sickly surreal,
some deny the danger, some fear future terrors.
If we glance back, we'll inspect the road's bend
for omens of chaos coming round.

In 1918, they trudged through mud and skeletal trees,
bodies seized by lice, blood, and tear gas.
As modern innovations streamlined the slaughter,
they lived in bedlam, named it
the Great, never seeing its sequel's beginnings.

The Nuremberg Laws restricted the Jews:
marked their cards with J's to stain their identities;
bleached their businesses by stealing and selling them
to Germans at bargain prices
—a plan reaching towards its full potential.

The bomb was birthed, and they fed it
lunch and dinner
to end the war. The peace is barely legible.
It sleeps in a bed of mutually assured destruction,
dreaming of feasting again.

Congress had extinguished the wish
to improve surveillance's sight,
but when the two towers crumbled,
the Patriot passed too quickly to consider
how it infringed on the rights of the people.

Time's always moving towards something more terrible.

## Dissonance

The others chat as I practice for our piano exam
It takes all my focus to hit the keys
at the right moment even with the metronome
turned up loud. I'm always late or early
to its tick-tick-tick—*she wouldn't vote for Obama,*
*but says he's a cool guy. That doesn't make sense*—

ticking. I slow the metronome, tap my hand
three ticks to get into the flow, and begin—
*If I knew they had voted for Trump,*
*I'd gone off on them*—dissonance sounds in my ears
when I ruin the chord with D instead of E.
My hands cramp in frustration, and the keys
look so slammable, but I've chosen
to not be angry. To overcome this. Move on. Let it be.

My first Thanksgiving since leaving for college
gives me the chance to show my family
my new skills, how I've grown, yet still fit
into the place I've always gone in in our puzzle.
When I'm done, the turkey isn't yet,
so we drift around other topics that slide in—*I think*
*he'll be a good president*—like waves pushing against
us lying on their surfaces.
Hungry and bored, I retreat to the piano
in the other room, hoping that time

will have allowed me to overcome
my frustration. I can't even touch the keys. I stare
at them as echoes bounce off canyons, thriving
in growing distance:

*good president*          *doesn't make sense.*

## Same Song, Second Verse

Back in your day, Thanksgiving was the reminder
as to why you avoid your family
the other 364.25 days of the year.
You can never find the key to lock your mouth
so you don't end up disputing their adorations
dressed in blindness
with your doomsday prophecies
in the booming voices that mark you
as blood brothers.

The kids kept their mouths quiet
as they withdrew into their phones,
chatting with the ones they chose,
their thumbs twiddling the hours,
the weeks, the months, the years away
till they could leave for college,
saying, *I'm never going backward.*

Once on their own,
they share their deepest
opinions with their friends,
revisit their favorite hot spots, and explore
what they were not allowed to see.
They peel back new floorboards,
for the first time not worrying
about how to sneak back into their house.
They chug down liberalism,
loosening their tongues
as they can no longer bear the unspoken
rants burning the back of their throats.
They smoke progressivism
till they are high enough to see the shape of the earth

and the heads of those who work the soil.
*Surely this must be the right way to see the world.*
They raise their voices to the tips
of their capital letters,
emphasize with exclamation marks,
add angry emojis for that secondhand rage.

When they return home easily ignited with new
lies, and you feel that your transmission is too weak
to break through the static of their echo chamber,
you say, *kids nowadays,* when they learned
these skills from the best at every Thanksgiving.

## Bound By Blood

Family reunions are so taxing
because we have to mingle with ones
we'd never choose to talk to.
As our differences glare at each other
from our shoulders, we sip our drinks
so our mouths are too full to retort.
Time has taught us how to keep from crashing
into those icebergs, ruining the whole vacation
by drowning everyone in frigid water.
(Though someone will probably fall asleep
at the wheel.)
Regardless, we gather together
to respect blood's tie.
We don't share our full selves
but rediscover basic commonalities—
our humanity and blood.
When I return to my cultures
of common passions, I'll always remember
the *just-one-more-minute*s spent here
as the only times
when people can still gather together
to retell one more story after one more story
and laugh at ourselves.

## Enduring Love

Growing up in church, I was given
'Be in the world, not of it' bread
and 'Love your neighbor' wine:
*Don't do drugs;*
*don't have premarital sex;*
*dress modestly.*

I took them without tasting their meaning.
The stale bread dissolved on my tongue
as the watered-down wine passed over.

I waited for this to become easy,
the happily ever after I'd been promised
once I had fallen in love with the Lord.

*Lay your troubles down,*
they sing.
*Be light with the joy he brings.*

Love.

So basic
because of how right it should feel.

But I never understood
till life directed me through the complexities
of what this Lord's love demanded:
that I must love even when they hurt me;
that I can wait, be silent;
deny myself what I deserve.

God did not bless me with my rights but with mercy.

Will I share it
without handing them a knife to cut me open?

I try to balance healthy boundaries
with openness for healing,
keep anger at a distance
though the wound is open.

There is nothing basic in what is beautiful.

When you are near, I swallow the rock
thump-thumping against its container.
It teaches

the pain of grace for every hurtful footfall
that treks forward towards nothing
with no care for crumpled leaves.

## The Sublime

I wish I could scream
this sorrow out of me,
but my flesh betrays me.
It crumbles useless
as it is brought life by this emotion
because my body is dead.
It shakes with unshed tears;
I cannot speak of the world's grief
that has pounded its way inside of me.

Around me, people worship you with exultant arms raised,
eyes closed and smiles gracing their singing lips:
*Holy Spirit, come abide within.*
*May Your joy be seen in all I do.*
But, trapped in my quivering rib cage,
all I know is pain.
I can't sing, I can't play, I can't dance.
I reach through my breaking
bricks, towards what's beyond, scared
it's going to destroy me.
I don't understand it.

It can't be mine.

## Inside the Mind of a Cashier (as if anyone would care)

*She went off on you 'cause she wants to feel important,*
my supervisor says to comfort me. I act like it's fine
because it is,
but I worry that he can see
the shaking beneath my walls,
see the replay of it,
>                of it,
>                        of it?
*These people are ridiculous.* We chuckle
with rolled eyes to temper our anger.
I'm just trying to do my job, and she dumps
the shit of her day on me. I'm hot and wired,
can't get the anger inside of me out. It crawls deep
into my mind to massage the chronic knot in my back.
I could say no, but I don't want to.
It whispers in my ear about that ex-friend
who acted like my victim,
though she had said what she knew would upset.
I'm thankful no one can hear my thoughts,
though I highly doubt any customer would notice
me dump the shit of my day on her memory.
Doesn't matter she's miles away
and five years since speaking. I'm stuck here
between Always Right and I Could Fire You.
College degree and pandemic later,
I'm scanning and tossing drawer knobs across my counter
harder than necessary. So many customers in line.
This never ends. Someone gives me a reason
to be annoyed, and I realize I'm still burning.
I've been craving this.

# 2 + 2 = 5

News has never been faker and the truth more lucrative,
or so it would seem.
The most valuable currency has always been belief.
Abigail Williams learned quickly
spells are cast with stories, not spice.
To save her skin,
burn another's.

As truth crumbled into individual's pieces,
wordsmiths peeled them from the streets,
but when they pieced them together,
the pages had yellowed and the ink faded.
It didn't matter. Out with the old, in with the new.
They knew the truth must end in a climax
to satisfy—that trembling *oh god I see everything now
how could I've not known this?*

The new age's headline became
*The Search for Truth: A Choose Your Own Facts Journey.*
The authors led their readers from the well
to the brackish stream, stroking
their hair as they spun their tales:

    *secret racist    smoke screen   microchips*
        *earth motionless       child sex slaves*

They said that one must cast off the most pervasive lies—
the ones most everyone believes—to be truly free.
We're all trying to outsmart Big Brother,
but he laughs,
because our search for an Orwellian nightmare
has created one.

## Visual Discourse

We see a flag, a statue, a color;
our hearts quicken at the sight of red.
We crouch down on the cusp of all we understand
but do not listen in case it begins to speak.

Those left behind after WWI
watched as sculptures of soldiers were erected.
Their shadows swallowed the ground
as they were moved to stand in the sun's glare,
showing onlookers their unfamiliar beauty:
finely chiseled lines of brows and muscles
they couldn't remember in their lanky boys;
elegant forms like Greek gods, symbolic of civility
—dying from disease in ditches.
Their gazes are forever set forward
in serenity like Jesus before his sacrifice
for the good of mankind.
They would not meet their families' eyes.

Their fight endures in our memory,
which favors the strong certainty of granite
over the weakness in flesh.
As past becomes history,
our fountain of knowledge flows penned lines,
black and murky—their last words
that they died for King God and Country.

## The Flag

What gives this piece of fabric its meaning?
From our lives we glean our understanding:
promises broken, freedoms worth the bleeding.
What gives this piece of fabric its meaning?
They disrespect dead brothers by kneeling.
They'd disrespect dead brothers by standing.
What gives this piece of fabric its meaning?
From our lives we glean our understanding.

## The Moral Equivalent of War

claimed Jimmy Carter
when oil was dangerously low.
He named the energy crisis
a national security threat
and called for vigilant sacrifice
by everyday soldiers,
listed 55 miles and 5-degree differences
in the people's ration books.
Hearing his words, Americans
rose to their responsibility to sacrifice
like their grandparents had done
during World War II.

# The Referent

The words hold a gifted power.
Their declaration echoed out
and formed one nation, one people.
All men are created equal.

The authors stepped just three-fifths in
so most would need more than statements
to taste the meat of the eagle.
All men are created equal.

They must fight to have its meaning
because their brothers aren't breathing.
Intention can be so fickle.
All men are created equal.

The words hold a gifted power.
All men are created equal.

# The Nationality of Dust

I'm American because I was born inside
this nation made from walls and war
not three centuries ago,
established on an earth
at least 200 million years old.
When my ancestors landed
on this soil, they could not shake off
the dust of their birth country. Their neighbors
called them Irish, Negroes turned inside out.
Now the same easily burned skin I wear
is called nothing. I'm American. Just American.
Race's line will bend if your looks are right.

Let's return to times before men with mud
depicted myths of creation on walls—
to when we were ungathered molecules
and all that existed in this earth were our beginnings.
Analyze these particles.
What is their nationality?

Does it make you sad when you think about
people going to hell?

Not really.
I don't dwell on it
—I can't—change
anything.
It's hard to open a door
that's been shut so long.

## Unclean

Jesus touched a corpse to make it clean
when the Jews only knew death to cause defilement,
not its cleansing by life.
The body's mother followed it out of town,

weeping, not thinking to ask that
Jesus touch a corpse to make it clean.
When it rose, a son, he clutched his mother,
his muscles strong and warm with life.

Raising hands, we stand on mountains to shout,
*Look and see that our actions are good—how*
*Jesus touched a corpse to make it clean.*
We paint our faces with righteous outrage

at others' sin so we are known by our fruits.
Their rotten innards gush under the Word weaponized
to bring death to defilement as we forget
Jesus touched a corpse to make it clean.

## Clean

See where I have not loved.
I have once been ignorant and will be again.
What I don't know
I fill with a thoughtless echo

of shallow claims and jokey barbs.
See where we have not loved.
When we address the other's prejudice,
we share our anger with our peers

rather than trying to change it.
We are all guilty. I hope that when you
see where I have not loved,
you will educate me with love, not shame.

I have judged safety based on race,
friendship on appearance, and have given
only the greetings I could do with ease.
See where I have not loved.

# Meaning

What is man that you are mindful of him;
        and the son of man that you visit him?

Stars age and die, ignorant of her.
Galaxies swirl around but do not
        perceive her presence.

It is you who gives him meaning,
        like man ascribes words meaning,
for he is the product of your word.

In this grand universe, you cared for her.
You clothed her in purpose
        within time's everlasting course.

What is man?
        That you are mindful of him.
And the daughter of man?
        That you come for her.

# For Those Who Feel Unworthy

Society tells us we must produce
a skill, a gift, a something that's unique
to us to then have worth. We can't be loved
just for existing in this universe.
We cannot look at one another as
our fellow human beings, say, *I love
you*, for we're taught that the unworthy are
deserving of disgust. But 'cause of their
humanity, they're worthy of our love.
Or, maybe none deserve it? What's our best
worth when the sun will swallow us? And yet,
a God came down to die for all and give
to us the love we didn't earn. Then we
should likewise give it to unworthy ones.

# Sight

It's easy for me to not see
the ugliness of this world
since I've only brushed against it—the tickle
of a whispered racist remark (low-key)
in the piece of Jackson, Mississippi that perches
on its edge like a white lady who's polite enough
till she wants to speak to the manager.
It's not surprising
because the occasional is normal—expected, even.

Overall, my peers are educated, kind, and believe
all deserve equality, so when people on TV cry victim
of racial injustice, I can't understand.
Who's doing it? I'm taught
the history that shows how far we've come
as I absentmindedly stroke the swirly, silver patterns
on the lid of America's jewelry box. We don't open it
as a rule
I learned
when I cracked it open an inch,
and they slammed it shut again. *That's not us*, we
say.
*That's not our America.*
*One nation,*
*under God,*

*with liberty and justice for all*[1].
I didn't try again

for one whiff of its stench was enough
and I wouldn't know how. They locked it and gave me
the head of the key—
classy, skeleton. I never saw the other part.
The jewelry box is on my desk
in the corner
where I throw loose papers
when I need an open space
to work. It's positioned so I can see it from bed,
sitting where the square window light is
off to the side
so the silver looks dull. You dust off
the essays, the tests—they crash to the floor

with the whipping sound of bent paper—so you can
trace the box's designs. *Did you know*
*that marijuana was criminalized as a way*
*to put black and queer people in jail?*
*They have Nixon*
*on tape*
*saying so.*

---

[1] Excerpt from a US History Textbook:

**Japanese Internment During WWII**

After the attack on Pearl Harbor, President Roosevelt
ordered the forced relocation of any Japanese in
America into concentration camps. Most were US
citizens. They were allowed to return to the West
Coast in 1945, three years later.

**The Invasion of Normandy**

It reminds me of the title of a book
*The New Jim Crow*
that I didn't give the chance.
*That sounds like a conspiracy. I*[2] *don't believe it.*


You move to place the jewelry box in my lap
but I press it back. *That's not our*[3] *America.*


You nod with the smile that tells me
you're about to say something you think is clever:
*because it is theirs,* and you present the body of my key.
It looks like a cross
with one side of the bottom half gnawed off.


As I hand you the key's head, I'm forced to accept
the jewelry box. Its cold body presses against
my crossed legs. The silver is flaking,
fiberglass underneath. As you twist the key's head on,
you explain: *Their America is the pool*
*on which we have constructed ours.*
*When the waves churn,*
*they splash to stain*
*our sidewalks.* You hold the completed key out.
*But you know how to avoid its puddles.*


I take it but don't move, staring at you.
I'm shaking.

---

[2] Privilege - the ability to believe what I want to
accept matters.
[3] Presupposition - a thing tacitly assumed beforehand
at the beginning of a line of argument or course of
action.
Example: "our America" presupposes that there is
another America not included in the one mentioned.

I don't want to see.

You guide my hand to unlock the box
and lift its lid.

## A Casual Comment

On a normal night in Indy,
all seems fine as we are walking
back to our hotel. Some figures,
a black woman and white cop in
front of us, begin bickering
and then yelling. We walk quicker
past them, running when the scene starts
to intensify. Before us,
one man says, *I hate those niggers.*

## As the Bell Continues to Toll

I closed my eyes and ears to lock in my sanity
and shut out the bell's screeching. I had to
to preserve the last strand of my innocence
before releasing it to the wind
once I accepted I couldn't hold on.
It's easy to ignore outside the bell house while asleep.
But you woke me and led me up the tower's stairs
into the keep where it swings.
Its momentum drags its dark, rust-stained body
through the air, and the beams overhead
creak as they flex with its weight.
Between the pillars, I look out into the world
and see a still life of a drowned toddler's body,
men debating what's to be done,
speculating whose fault it is.
Death tolls and death threats scroll across the bottom.
*You cannot ignore this.*

The bell rings of hate that festers in computer chips,
of fear strangling a new-world orphan in detainment.
As the bell tolls—louder—louder—I am forced
to swallow it
and live with it inside my chest. Its sound aches
my bones till they shake, knocking my knees together,
and I fall.
I rest against a pillar,
but the bell reverberates through the stone.

Why should I exist unburdened
when there's so much to mourn?
Sanity should be my sacrifice.
                                        But

I don't think it's wrong to clasp
the loving times to keep myself together:
his embrace so tight it imbued its strength in me;
her patience when I grew frustrated,
frayed by my depression;
when he told me not to be ashamed of all my tears
for they're a gift from you to show your truth.

Though the bell diminishes me, these moments
will give me strength to love, to hope, to fight
for what justice I can bring with my deeds.

## Teaching Terror

*I want my mom,* I said as legs walked past me.
My need for her pressed me
against the brown beadboard
as the metal building of my elementary school
stretched. The hallway became infinite, the upstairs
unreachable.
I know now it was a small building,
but any space becomes big enough
to swallow someone when your fear unravels
your ability to move.
I pleaded with giants to give her back,
and when she returned, I'd like to say I was lucky
to have been reunited with her,
but you can't get lucky
when nothing was ever truly amiss.

And that fear is nothing compared__

I can't imagine what it's like__

Can't you see that it's wrong__

I write poetry
not for people to echo my melody back to me,
but to ask them to do the most dangerous thing
—to question themselves.
I know this fear. It devours
your words, your identity, your stability, your faith.
You don't know where it will stop.

I've toiled over these poems in the hope
that the right words, the right intention,
the right argument will get you to listen,

but I can't do it for this.
I shouldn't even have to talk about it. Like,
how is this a thing?
I can't find the words
because there should be none

for how awful
it is

to keep migrant children in cages
as their world stretches, infinite and scary,
their parents unreachable, with no guarantee
that they will ever know their embrace again,

only terror.

## We were not cut, so we were not scarred

My Facebook feed is full of profile changes
from cute official couple pics to selfies
of smiling white faces framed
by "I stand with refugees."
They change like posters on a college bulletin board.
Papers protesting the racist monument
on the town square
that we pass on our way to get ice cream
are covered in a few weeks
by $869 a month! Large living room! Open floor plan!
Don't miss the Open Mic Night next Thursday!
Meanwhile, a black man prepares for his march
against the monument
every Sunday evening for the nineteenth year.

## But America's One of the Best Nations in the World

Above you stands the Statue of Liberty
that has watched over countless immigrants
as they made their first steps towards
the coveted American dream.
Her torch shines so brightly
that vagrants march through violence
and climb over walls
to reach her rusted copper body.
Unlike them,
you and I may romp in this bed of opportunity
because it's made by our fathers' work.
Enjoy its class mobility,
refrigerated offerings, shoes,
and comforters.
You don't even have to emerge
from them to change the channel
from parents mourning
the victims of the latest shooting.
And if ever there's a moment
when you're bored,
don't hesitate to watch sex
made with flesh
priced and purchased
at your convenience.
And don't forget
our most treasured offering: freedom.
You have a wide selection to choose from
that include, but are not limited to:
freedom of religion;
freedom of speech;
freedom of protest, except

in the cases of protesting the police;
freedom to bear a lethal weapon;
freedom to choose your rulers
from a select few of wealthy individuals
who are often mistaken for pathological liars;
and finally, freedom to put your beliefs
over others' lives by not wearing masks
and only listening to opinions that agree with your own
no matter how much your inaction harms
those who are less fortunate.

Welcome to America: where you can hide
from poverty and disease
but not from human nature.

## Patriotism

I can't remember the pride
of being privileged with this heritage.
It was a fact I'd taken for granted
till time took it from me.

## Allegiance

I pledge allegiance to the flag
of the United States of America,
and to the Republic for which it stands,
one nation, indivisible,
with liberty and justice for all.

I pledge allegiance
to the United States of America,
and to the Republic for which it stands,
one nation under God, indivisible,
with liberty and justice for all.

I pledge allegiance
to the            States of America,
and to the Republic for which it stands,
one nation under God, indivisible,
with liberty and justice for

I pledge allegiance
to                      America,
and to the Republic for which it stands,
     nation    God, indivisible,
with liberty and justice for its citizens.

one          God
with liberty and justice for its citizens

   pledge allegiance
to                      America
       to                    stand
          for God,

                          who

   pledges allegiance
to                         America,
and to the men
one true nation-God, indivisible,
with     allegiance         for all

                                              who


   pledge allegiance to the flag
and to the Republic
only nation under God

                  God's nation       divisible,
           from all.

I pledge allegiance
              one


               America


          one     God.

## The Conservative Gospel

Blessed are you when people hate you
because of the Son of Man.
The True King will rescue
his children who follow his commands.

Because of the Son of Man,
the Romans burned and crucified
his children who followed his commands,
and God blessed them for their faith.

The Romans burned and crucified
but couldn't crush their conviction.
God blessed them for their faith
—a land free from any ruler

who could crush their conviction.
But rivers of gold and a new chance at nobility
in this land free from any ruler
corrupted their past peace.

Rivers of gold and a new chance at nobility
chipped at their convictions, and a new voice
corrupted their past peace
with a revolution of sexual freedom and equality.

It chipped at their convictions, and the new voice
despised them for their old values, incompatible
with a revolution of sexual freedom and equality.
Radio voices painted them as fanatical,

despised for their religious values, incompatible
with any policy put forward by Democrats.

Radio voices painted them as fanatical:
*They hate God and will attack*

*with any policy put forward by Democrats.*
*They stand on stages, mic'd up, praised*
*for hating God and attacking*
*you. They justify their actions, unafraid.*

So Christians stand on stages, mic'd up, and praise
Caesar who will rescue
them. They justify their actions, unafraid:
*Blessed are you when people hate you.*

# To the Street Preacher Who Doesn't Believe in Science

What God wants is us to study all
the exquisite particles he called
into being—puzzle pieces
meant to show a hidden beauty—pages
where he wrote his vision for the world:

us united to each other and enthralled
by him. But the speeches you sculpt
claim that tyrannical obedience is
what he wants.

You deny creation to exalt
the creator and from your pedestal
tell of the god you forget came from heavens
to live with us, as us and promised
love. How can your rants be at all
what he wants?

# The Third Commandment

Every use of a word mutates its meaning.
>America has turned away from God.
It collects the associations, the emotions, the ideas,
>God          Hates          Fags.
expressed in every context, in every argument,
>Jesus wouldn't wear a mask.
in every ideology.
>America has forsaken godly, conservative
>values.


The listeners shoved words down their throats
>whoever does not take up their cross
>and follow me is not worthy of me.
without tasting them, and puked them up,
half-decomposed.
>Blessed are you when you offend others.
They ran ahead with crosses blazing
>to put to death some who should not die.
and threw out the charred remains of mercy
when they no longer fed their fires.


In 2020 C. E., people knelt at the table of science,
rationality, humanism without the creator of them,
for they had so often found his fruits
in the mouths of deniers, wedged between
the teeth of conspiracy and bigotry.
>You have profaned me
>by your lying to my people
>who listen to lies.


As the world ended, no one named Emmanuel,
for his name had been used so many times

its meaning had changed.

I AM WHO I AM.

## A Lamp Under A Jar

After the court voted to protect
same-sex marriage, you proclaimed
on Facebook that our nation had turned
from God. I stayed silent.
It's good you want to stand for him, but perhaps
pointing words at an other is the safer opposition
we need in order to sleep well.
I don't want to wake you,
because you look so peaceful, alone in your bed
under your eagle feather, silk duvet.
But if we wanted the whole time
to close our eyes and dream,
we shouldn't have told him
to sign our names in the book of life.
For by grace we have been saved through faith
—but it comes with a

price: to act justly, love mercy, walk humbly
with God. But we've told the poor
the tide is coming
and not given them our bread.
When the system slips whole lives
down its gullet, we've excused ourselves
from the table. How many times
can we refuse others' disruptions
till God no longer recognizes
us—the stand upon which his light should show?
Did the first Christians expect to fulfill this promise
by their bodies being burned to give the night light?
We're all meant to die,
one way or another,
to gain life. The weight of what he will ask

is terrifying. I don't blame you for being scared.
I tremble
as I stand in the shadows, hearing bells.
In the face of his commands, I'm so weak
that it's the greatest effort to open my eyes
and speak.

## Zombie, what's in your head?

I was never the same after
we spilled blood over inanimate representations
of dead men—men birthed from propaganda,
who never existed.
I don't think we
were the same.
Except that's not true.
We've been like this.

The bell has never stopped tolling.
It has just screeched so long it rings
in our teeth, the toothache we've gotten used to
mostly. 'Cause it's not us.
It's not our families

who are dying. I sit in the grass
because my legs can't support the burden
of my own uselessness. Beneath,
the soil is unforgiving. Scratching at it
only gives me a handful,
but I need it.
When I am holding dirt, I am holding men.
Man, woman,
black, white,
I cannot tell.

I look forward
into the valley of the future as you come
to stand over me. I wonder

now that we can smell the reek
of what we've wrought,

do you still think of those stone men
that made you strike our brother's cheek?

## Listening to a Person Scream

This world,
its death
can only be bearable if we shove it into a corner, focus
on the solution instead of feeling it, keep it behind
closed friendships, sleep it off, it'll be fine, time heals
all wounds, but time always leads to death and the
intimacy of this pain has been torn out for public
display because how could anyone keep quiet the
ripping of one's skin to make muscle their clothing.

Sometimes
I wish
that instead of debating how to fix things
or whose right is it anyway
that we would just sit in the sorrow for a moment.

Maybe that is too much to ask.
To sit there
as the drill of dread approaches like a rat burrowing into your
intestines to escape the heat—faster—further—and the
vertigo of your body expands while your mind's stationary
cause the only way out is through.

## How the Poet Endeavored to Explain Language's Influence on our Comprehension of the World

Times New Roman double-spaced never loses
a staring match. I bury my face
into the mattress in shame. I have
six more weeks to finish my bachelor's,

the world is falling apart, and I don't know
how to convince my paper's non-existent audience
to believe me. My professor claimed
truth wasn't enough. You must frame it

in a way that people will accept. Surrendering
to distraction, I scroll Instagram past anxious urgings
to stay home because lockdowns are effective,
look, China has the pandemic under control.

I give up. On my way downstairs, the TV
in my parents' bedroom spouts out
that these corona tweets are Chinese propaganda.
Doctors and nurses fight on the front lines,

but the US won't declare war like on
poverty and drugs because it can't be
fought with militarized police or money.
Downstairs, I read *Flatland.* The square

cannot comprehend the idea of a sphere
though he had called the king of Lineland a fool
for the same thing a chapter earlier.
The sphere squeezes itself through his world,

but the circle only grows and shrinks
because there is no tall. Square says,
*I don't understa—bing.* I have a new email.
My pastor warns us of the politicization

of everything. People knead life
till it must shed its complexities
into something easy to comprehend.
When I told my sister I don't identify

with the political spectrum, she named me
a moderate. It flattens all my beliefs,
experiences, and contradictions
into a dot on a one-dimensional line
or a slightly more comprehensive
second-dimensional compass. But the frame will
break if you sho-
ve too much in.
In the end,
the sphere has to snatch Square
from his dimension
for him
to understand.

## Sonnet 18: Covid Edition

Shall I compare your actions to your words?
You threw a Christmas party, Tate Reeves,
once you were done entreating us to avert
the spread of the disease by forgoing family.
I've not forgotten you, Newsom, for one
three-household ban later, you celebrated
a birthday. And while the essential front
of workers waited, Pence demonstrated
for them his faith in vaccines, having avoided
masks or quarantining. They placed their bets
that time would keep on going and erode
the moments not great enough to make history. But,
so long as men can breathe, or eyes can see,
so long lives these words that'll give life to memory.

## The Record's Scratched

Love your country, vote, pledge allegiance to the flag,
exercise your rights, your freedom, and individuality
are all answers to the question never asked—
How can someone be proud of being an American?
Stand up every morning in middle school
to declare your allegiance,
launder your family's flag, exercise your freedom
to read about corrupt governments
that controlled their people
with secret police, doublethink and division,
be taught the unbelievable history of colonies
that took the opportunities of a new world
and made itself into a superpower
of small towns, simple times, wealth, consumerism,
dreams, and the fight to give every man the right
to vote, make a poster for a school project to advertise
voting between a woman and the man who campaigns
on the fear of how can someone be proud
of being an American when the world laughs at us
for our passivity? Remember:
we are the best nation in the world;
we are better than China, than Russia,
than the third world, than the second,
because we are the first to declare independence
against tyranny, to land on the moon, to make
the atomic bomb, to make itself great. Again,
love your country because of the freedom
it gives you to vote for whomever says what you want
to hear, the pride it gives you to be part of the best,
better than fascists who committed genocide,
than commies who killed dissenters,
learn the unbelievable history of the massacre

71

of African Americans in Tulsa by deputized
whites, learn how the government uses fake news
and division to control, turn on the two-minute hate:
illegals taking our jobs, a deputized white
kneeling a black man into death, his onlookers out
on bail, the best healthcare system in the world
strained to its breaking point
because we value our freedom,
our individuality more than life.
The celebrity president says it's all a hoax.
Hospitalization data sent to the executive branch,
supplies cut, only crazies would defund, states
should handle it, national guard sent out,
less help, more force,
police shove peaceful protesters into unmarked vans,
refugees return to violent homes because
the camps of the promised land are contaminated
by chemicals, moldy food, and disappearing children.
How can someone be proud of being an American
when this country is fa—
                    —scist?
According to Google, signs of a fascist nation include,
but are not limited to, powerful nationalism, disdain
for human rights, unification through identifying an
enemy, obsession with national security, crime and
punishment, controlled mass media. How
            can     be proud        of
        American.      Remember:    better
    than China —
        —   don't reeducate    detainees
    than Nazi            don't gas    —
            —displacing children   genocide.
        Russia,     dissenters—
            —   released after    short

72

## Justice and Violence

We have a curfew now
because it's not safe.
It's to keep the riots and looting
from plundering our city
like in others
where BLM protesters and the police
destroy buildings and bones
day and night. Day and night.
Some spectators justify their cries,
saying this is the fate
of a nation who oppresses its people,
that the rich and the powerful
deserve this destruction.
I, like my predecessors,
point to Martin Luther King Jr.
as the poster boy for the usefulness
of peaceful protests,
forgetting he was shot in the face.
His followers' peaceful cries
had to be met with violence
to be heard
and move the hearts of many.
But from the sidelines,
their brothers and sisters
couldn't wait and watch,
so they took up arms to give
the other its due
day and night. Decade and century.
For decades and centuries.
Every right we have is written in blood.

## The Rat Race for Utopia

Sitting around the fire/radio/television/computer,
Uncle listens to his world, growing grimmer,
and grieves the life he could not live
and the one his children will have to
if his grandchildren are to live the life he could not live.
He pats his son's head
as he plays with his sticks/doll/paper planes/phone.
*Maybe you will fix what I could not,* he thinks.
*My generation's beliefs have ossified like our bones.*

When the son grows up, he fights
with spears/swords/guns/bombs to drag change
into the next age. It kicks and screams,
demolishing the old to bring forth
a new king/nation/government/dictator,
till it hibernates in a bed of new hopes
where oppression rises and falls on the backs
of following generations, all longing
for the redemption that will come
                and stay.

## Under Derek Chauvin's Knee

The earth crammed itself down against its fault
till it burst forward. Cracks stranded children
from their parents as cliffs of silence fell
into the sea. The earth pushed up square miles
of #JusticeforFloyd, marching feet, and shocked
tears into a swell that from the shore looked
strong enough to wash the police system away,
but after the months it took to travel, it laps tired
against my feet. I stand my ground in an effort
to sink but only get up to my ankles
before the shifting sand forces me to move
on. When I kick and push to splash up my own
waves, another one slam-dunks me down,
so I return home, worn out and called out by a meme
of throwing a bicycle of Change.org petitions
at an armored car of problems.

# I don't know how to do any of this

I'm crying in the Bed, Bath, and Beyond parking lot
because you don't understand what God has told me.
Over the phone, we swap fears
and tell of what we see through the molted glass
when we look at Trump:
Fascism            Freedom
    at Biden:
Hope               Venezuela.
Didn't our therapists and God tell us
we can't know what the future holds?

We've read the scriptures, we've prayed,
and found through Spirit God-given answers:
Not Trump        Trump.
One of us must be deceived
because why would one God give two answers?

I'm not wrong. Believe me; I would change
my mind if I could because I know how good
it would taste to be of one mind with my family again
rather than alone, and I can only change myself.
But I can't lie. Have you considered it?

Once we hang up, I resume my day
to shop for curtains and cutlery, feeling wasted
on emotion. That night, we read the scriptures,
*And if I have all faith, so as to remove mountains,*
*but have not love, I am nothing.* I don't know how
to hold conviction and love in the same hand
though God has given me both.
My fingers cramp. I'm sure to drop one.

## Another Attempt

I sit on the couch, my hair tangled,
my face sticky with sleep oil,
my apartment's curtains drawn, weighted
by the wait for an answer. Why
has everything gone wrong?
The phone in my lap is my door to the outside world
because I can't walk out without a mask. I can't talk
to anyone. It is large enough to only filter in the bad.
What am I to do? College would give me the answer,
they said, and when I continued confused,

I clutched the desire to do what God wanted.
Surely, that future would be good
since it's the only place to find fulfillment.
Change strapped itself to my shoulders.
There is so much love and sorrow
in it that I have to get out. My pretty words stare back
at only me, though, as the bell continues to toll.
*Act justly, love mercy, walk humbly with God.*
He has come to redeem this dumpster fire,

and what am I to do when I am his hand, his foot,
his mouth? I was terrified
of proving false like those I grew up around
who fought for football teams, not for justice;
of the fire of my faith crumbling under the banality
of making a good life for myself, not for others.
I twisted my life to reflect what it should—
volunteered for a yearlong mission
—so work would prove my faith
true. I must run hard
to pursue his work

(and outpace my sin). Sacrifice
my time, my money, my passions, my friends,
the home I've unintentionally created
where I have been—privileges
I should not treasure if others lack them.
What am I to do? Here is my/their answer
so I no longer have to fear the shame of unknown,
until

corona treads through bodies to make my plans
into a viper that I twist and twist
into a knot, but it will never
form what it ought to be. The phone in my lap
is my door to the outside world; the key locks it.
An email tells me there will be no mission,
no purpose. I tried to do what God wanted
—he told me to go.
I obeyed, so why did this happen?

When I look into the future, I see
nothing. A plague
has stripped the altar of my life and left me
with the terror of living. If I stay here,
did I not truly care?
My phone is my door to the outside world. It is small
enough to only filter in questions. *What are we to do?*
When an officer suffocates a black man with his knee,
there is no calling the police. This world
is a dumpster fire,
and we are hands, we are feet, we are a mouth
that must not be silent, but we don't know how to heal
suffering that has been centuries in the making.
We will tear the buildings down,

the words out of mouths, the thoughts out of minds
because this pain cannot go on any longer
now that we know it. Unfollow us, we challenge,
if that moment, that video, that summer
did not rip out the roots of everything
you thought you knew
from their quiet life in the dirt.　　　　But,
time kept going. And the officer got out on bail,
and there are still many more centuries
for the world to suffer,
many more days to exist in the soil. Most of change
is done in the growing—in the putting
something of yourself into the ground,
tending to it everyday, hoping the seed produces fruit,
though sometimes it doesn't.

What am I to do, God?

What are we to do?

I just wanted to do what God wanted of me,
so I led my Isaac up the mountain. As I raised a knife,
with a great tragedy, God grabbed my wrist
and said: *to do righteousness and justice*
*is more acceptable to me than sacrifice.*

When months pass and I take a walk
on a warm winter day,
I still feel weighted by the wait of a year
that feels like a waste
because I'm not going anywhere.
What do you want me to do, God?
Where am I meant to be?

I stop walking. Here

is as good of an answer as I'll get.
There is no great aha reveal
to what my life's been marching towards
'cause most of life is done in the living
—in the getting up to brush my hair,
in the day's work, in the late nights
that build into relationships,
and in the long seasons it takes to grow.
I'm not sure how to live
while carrying this knapsack of sorrow,
hope, and responsibility for this dumpster fire,
but maybe an answer is not the point.
Maybe, I just need to trek up the mountain
so he may grab my hand.

# Thy Will Be Done

"Continue in the fear of the Lord all day."

I wash my hands and pray like I've been taught:

*Our Father who art in Heaven, hallowed be thy name,*
*thy kingdom come, thy will be done.*
*Please, God, protect*
*me and my family from getting corona*
*over these holidays. Lord, heal*
*our nation. Please, open our eyes to the truth*
*that we need you during this time. Comfort*
*those who are sick and dying*
*and their families who grieve. Reconcile*
*us because we've let politics divide us.*
*Please God, give me strength*
*to get through this year and have mercy on us.*
*Thank you.*
*Amen.*

When history makes itself around you, it's normal
to want to see your place in the books. I see it now,
hidden between the lines
connecting big event after big event.
It is in life bridging the gaps between memories,
like when I came home from work
on 10/27/20 at 4:25pm,
sat in my car to watch children walk from school,
carrying backpacks, textbooks in hands,
masks slid down under their chins
as our nation changed
around us. Voting and hospitalizations records
broken, climbing,

while the president files court case after court case
to veto his people, while guns and ammo
run out of stock.

The future has never felt so terrible,
because death and destruction have never felt so
inevitable.
I can't stop it,

so I wash my hands, and I pray:

*Our Father*
        *thy will be done.*
*Please, God, protect*
*me and my family.*
                *Lord, heal*
*our nation.        open our eyes*
        *we need you*
                        *Reconcile*
*us*
*Please God, give me strength*
        *have mercy on us.*

I can vote but I can't choose who will win
or what they and their people will do.
I wash my hands,
but I may still get sick, and I'm going to die.
The virus spirals closer. How much longer
can I remain untouched? Or will I always sit
in my car, see more police as I drive around, then
watch the leaves turn orange for another year,
go home, prepare for work the next day,
wash my hands, and pray:

*Please, God*

                    *Lord*

        *Please*

  *have mercy on us.*

      *Please*          *God*

                     *Please*

"Surely there is a future, and your hope will not be cut off."

                    - Proverbs 23:17b-18

# Acknowledgments

Writing a poetry collection is hard. Writing any book is hard, and this collection would not be what it is without the following people:

Thank you to *Bridge: The Bluffton Literary Journal* for including "10,000 Hours" in their Fall 2021 edition.

Thank you to the University of North Texas Writing Club, Professor Raina Joines, and to my friends Alex Sten and Brendon James for taking the time to read these poems and provide feedback. A second pair of eyes is necessary to fully see any written work. Thank you for lending me yours.

Thank you to Alejandrob for providing an amazing cover and Ksproofingpower for making sure I don't embarrass myself with proofreading errors.

Thank you to my parents, the Village Church Denton, and my linguistic professors for everything you have taught me. The conversations we have shared have changed my life and inspired this work.

And lastly, thank you to Jesus, my Lord and Savior, for dying on the cross for my sins. I hope these words please you.